Biff's First Times Tables

Written by Roderick Hunt

Illustrated by Alex Brychta

OXFORD
UNIVERSITY PRESS

Biff and Chip are twins.

"We'll soon be seven," said Chip. "If we each have a cake, how many candles will we need?"

"Times tables can help," said Dad. "There will be 7 candles on each cake. There are 2 cakes. So you will need 14 candles altogether."

7 × 2 = 14

"Who is coming to your birthday party?" asked Dad.

"Wilf and Wilma," said Biff.

1 × 2 = 2

"And Kipper and Anna, that's 4."

2 × 2 = 4

"Nadim and Anneena, makes 6."

3 × 2 = 6

"And Craig and Chang, is 8."

4 × 2 = 8

"We need 8 goody bags," said Biff. "We'll put 2 toys in each one. That's 8 times 2, so we need 16 toys."

This is my 2 times table.

1 × 2 = 2
2 × 2 = 4
3 × 2 = 6
4 × 2 = 8
5 × 2 = 10
6 × 2 = 12
7 × 2 = 14
8 × 2 = 16
9 × 2 = 18
10 × 2 = 20

Chip planned a game for the party. "There are 10 children, so we need 2 teams of 5," he said.

Team A	Team B
Chip	Biff
Chang	Craig
Wilma	Wilf
Anneena	Anna
Kipper	Nadim

$2 \times 5 = 10$

"Mum and Dad are hiding 6 eggs for each person. There are 5 people in each team. So, each team needs to find 30 eggs!" said Chip.

$$6 \times 5 = 30$$

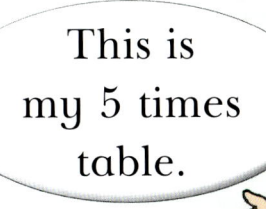

This is my 5 times table.

1 × 5 = 5
2 × 5 = 10
3 × 5 = 15
4 × 5 = 20
5 × 5 = 25
6 × 5 = 30
7 × 5 = 35
8 × 5 = 40
9 × 5 = 45
10 × 5 = 50

The twins went shopping with Mum. They bought 2 mini pizzas for each of the 10 children at the party.

$$2 \times 10 = 20$$

And 4 strawberries for each child.

$$4 \times 10 = 40$$

"Chip's cake looks so good, I could eat six slices," joked Craig.

"If we all ate 6," said Biff, "that would be 60 slices!"

6 × 10 = 60

> This is my 10 times table.

$1 \times 10 = 10$

$2 \times 10 = 20$

$3 \times 10 = 30$

$4 \times 10 = 40$

$5 \times 10 = 50$

$6 \times 10 = 60$

$7 \times 10 = 70$

$8 \times 10 = 80$

$9 \times 10 = 90$

$10 \times 10 = 100$

It is very useful to learn all the times tables.

1 × 3 = 3	1 × 4 = 4	1 × 6 = 6
2 × 3 = 6	2 × 4 = 8	2 × 6 = 12
3 × 3 = 9	3 × 4 = 12	3 × 6 = 18
4 × 3 = 12	4 × 4 = 16	4 × 6 = 24
5 × 3 = 15	5 × 4 = 20	5 × 6 = 30
6 × 3 = 18	6 × 4 = 24	6 × 6 = 36
7 × 3 = 21	7 × 4 = 28	7 × 6 = 42
8 × 3 = 24	8 × 4 = 32	8 × 6 = 48
9 × 3 = 27	9 × 4 = 36	9 × 6 = 54
10 × 3 = 30	10 × 4 = 40	10 × 6 = 60

Here are the rest!
How many do you know?

1 × 7 = 7	1 × 8 = 8	1 × 9 = 9
2 × 7 = 14	2 × 8 = 16	2 × 9 = 18
3 × 7 = 21	3 × 8 = 24	3 × 9 = 27
4 × 7 = 28	4 × 8 = 32	4 × 9 = 36
5 × 7 = 35	5 × 8 = 40	5 × 9 = 45
6 × 7 = 42	6 × 8 = 48	6 × 9 = 54
7 × 7 = 49	7 × 8 = 56	7 × 9 = 63
8 × 7 = 56	8 × 8 = 64	8 × 9 = 72
9 × 7 = 63	9 × 8 = 72	9 × 9 = 81
10 × 7 = 70	10 × 8 = 80	10 × 9 = 90

How many balloons are there altogether? 4 × 2 = ?

How many presents are there altogether? 4 × 5 = ?

How many eggs are there altogether?   5 × 6 = ?

10 cakes each have 7 candles. How many candles are there altogether?   10 × 7 = ?

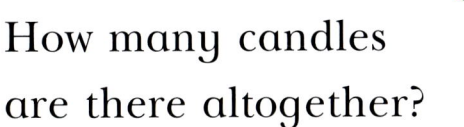

Talk about the times tables

What do times tables help us to do?

Biff and Chip are twins. How old are they?

How many friends came to their party?

Say one of the times tables you have learnt.